The Usborne Piano Course

Book Two

Katie Elliott and Kathy Gemmell

Original music and arrangements by Katie Elliott

Illustrated by Simone Abel

Designed by Sarah Bealham

Design consultant: Russell Punter

Edited by Emma Danes

Series editor: Anthony Marks

Music reminders

Before you play a tune, remember to look for the signs that tell you about it. These are just as important as the notes.

Can you answer these questions about the tune below? Check your answers on page 32.

Brother, come and dance with me

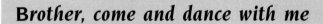

Don't forget...

2

Looking at notes

In this book, you will learn new notes in both the treble and bass clefs. When you learn a new note, make sure you look carefully at where it sits on the staff.

Is it on a line or in a space?

Here is what all the notes in the treble clef are called.

These notes all sit in spaces.

These notes are all on lines.

Here are all the notes in the bass clef.

All these notes are in spaces.

All these notes are on lines.

How many of these notes can you find and play on your piano?

Remembering notes

You can use the names of the notes on the lines and in the spaces to make words or sentences.

1. The notes in the treble-clef spaces spell FACE (from the bottom up).

2. For the notes on lines, make up a sentence using words starting with E, G, B, D and F.

E, G, B, D, F,...
...Every Green Bus Drives Fast.

3. Make up a sentence using the first letters of the bass-clef notes in spaces...

4. ...and another for the notes on the lines.

A, C, E, G...
...All Cows Eat Grass.

G, B, D, F, A...
...Granny Bakes Doughnuts For All.

These are just ideas. Can you make up some funny sentences of your own to help you remember which note is which?

Rests

Music often has silent parts where one or both hands have to stop playing. These silent parts are called rests.

Rests last for different numbers of beats, just like notes. There are different signs for rests of different lengths.

Where a whole bar is silent, a semibreve rest is used, whatever the length of the bar.

Clapping

Try clapping this rhythm. Remember to leave a gap every time you see a rest.

Happy Hoppy

4

Loud, quiet and silent

Look out for the signs in this tune that tell you how loudly or quietly to play. Don't forget to lift your fingers off the keys for the rests.

Remember, *f* is for forte which means "play loudly".

p is for piano which means "play quietly".

Bobby Shaftoe

A new hand position

In the next tune, there are three new bass-clef notes for the left hand.

Below, you can see where they are on the staff and their positions on the keyboard.

This note, E, sits in the second space from the top.

This note, D, is on the middle line.

This note, C, sits in the second space up.

C D E   Middle C

To play these notes, you need to move your left hand down the keyboard.

Think of your funny sentences to help you remember which note is which.

Granny Bakes Doughnuts For All ...G B D F A

Move your thumb from Middle C down to the G below.

L.H.   Middle C

Jingle Bells

Start on the third finger of your left hand.

This tune was written by a man called Pierpont.

Merry-go-round

Music quiz

The answers are on page 32.

Can you remember the names of all these notes?

What is this sign called and what does it mean?

What does this sign tell you to do?

Helter Skelter

Shorter notes

The next tune has a note in it that is shorter than any you have played so far. It is called a quaver.

This is a quaver. It lasts for half a crotchet beat.

When there are two quavers next to each other in a bar, their tails are often joined together.

Here are two quavers joined together.

Porridge

This tune is easier than it looks. Both hands do the same thing all the way through.

More about quavers

What are quavers worth?

A new time signature

The tune below uses a new time signature. It has a two on top.

See if you can clap these bars, counting two crotchet beats in each bar.

The bee

A quiet tune: *Drifting*

This is a very peaceful tune, so play it *piano* (quietly). You can either play it by yourself, or with someone else playing the accompaniment on the opposite page.

Make sure you take your fingers slightly off the keys during the rests.

Playing together

Once you know "Drifting" on page 10, you can try playing it with this accompaniment.

Ask someone who is good at the piano to play this tune at the same time as you play your part on the opposite page.

Drifting (accompaniment)

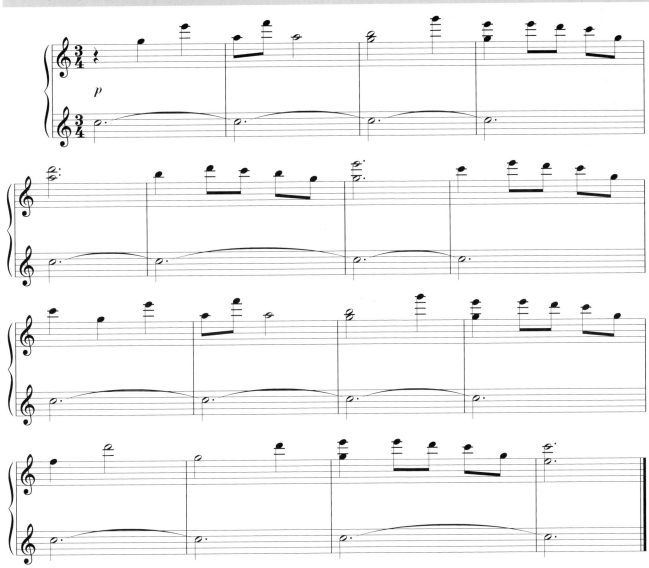

Your first black key

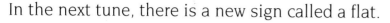

In the next tune, there is a new sign called a flat.

This is a flat sign.

A flat sign comes before a note on the same space or line. It makes the note sound slightly lower.

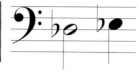

The new note in the tune below is for your left hand. It is called B flat. To find

B flat on your piano, first find B, then play the black key just to its left.

This is B flat. Play it with the second finger of your left hand.

B flat is often written like this:

Can you find other B flats on your piano?

Bb

B   Middle C

How flats work in a tune

A flat sign can affect more than one note. When a B becomes a B flat, all the Bs after it in that bar change to B flat as well.

When you start a new bar, the Bs will not change to B flats unless there is another flat sign before one of them.

You play B flat.

You play B flat here because there is a B flat earlier in this bar.

Here you play ordinary B. There is no B flat in this bar.

Buzzing around

Remember, play B flat if there is a flat sign before the B...

... or if there is a B flat earlier in the bar.

Semitones

B flat sounds a little lower than ordinary B. The distance beween B and B flat is called a semitone.

From here...

...to here is a semitone.

A semitone is the smallest distance between two notes on a keyboard.

From here...

...to here is a semitone.

From here...

...to here is a semitone.

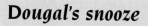

Dougal's snooze

Remember to play B flat if a B earlier in the same bar has been lowered a semitone to B flat.

Look out for the repeat in this tune.

Play this tune *piano* (quietly).

Moving up

In the next tune, there are three new treble-clef notes for your right hand.

Look at where to find them on the staff and where they are on the piano.

This note, A, sits in the second space up from the bottom.

This note, B, is on the middle line of the staff.

This note, C, sits in the second space from the top.

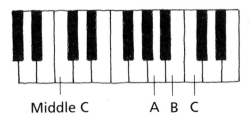

Middle C   A B C

To play these notes, you need to move your right hand up the piano.

Move your thumb from Middle C...

...to the F above Middle C.

Middle C

R.H.

Play A with your third finger.

Play B with your fourth finger.

Play C with your fifth finger (your little finger).

Think back to the sentences you made up on page 3 to help you remember which note is which in the treble clef.

The next tune will help you get used to playing with your hand in this new position.

Wagtails

B flat in the right hand

In the next tune, all the Bs in the right hand have become B flats.

Like the last tune, you will need to play this one with your hand in its new position.

Instead of putting your fourth finger on B, put it on B flat, the black key immediately to its left.

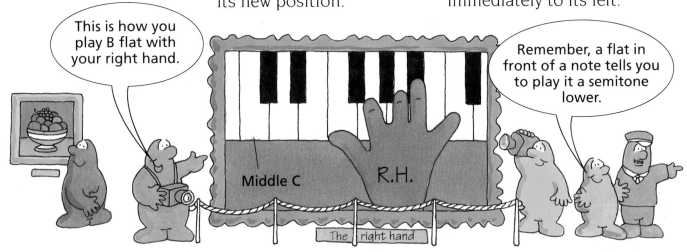

This is how you play B flat with your right hand.

Middle C

R.H.

The right hand

Remember, a flat in front of a note tells you to play it a semitone lower.

Humming song

Practise playing B flat with the fourth finger of your right hand a few times before you play this tune.

This tune was written by a German called Schumann.

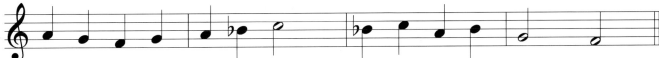

Note finding

Can you say the names of all these notes? You can see if you got them right on page 32.

15

Sight-reading hints

Remember to look for clues about a tune before you play it.

Is it for both hands to play...

...or just one hand?

How many beats are there in each bar?

Are there any signs telling you to play *forte* (loudly)...

...or *piano* (quietly)?

Girls and Boys

Remember that a flat sign at the beginning of a bar...

...changes all the Bs to B flats in that bar.

Looking sharp

There is a new sign written before some of the notes in the next tune. It is called a sharp.

A sharp sign makes the note following it a semitone higher. A sharp is the opposite of a flat, which makes a note a semitone lower.

Ho la hi

Look out for the F sharps in this tune. Play them with the fourth finger of your right hand.

Sharper still

This tune has a left hand F sharp in it. Move your left thumb from Middle C down to B. Play F sharp with your fourth finger.

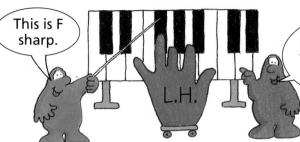

This is F sharp.

You don't play any ordinary Fs in this tune, so you can keep your fourth finger over F sharp.

Chiapenecas

This is a Mexican tune. First practise playing F sharp with your fourth finger.

Remember that a sharp sign affects all the Fs which follow it in the same bar.

18

Flats and sharps

In the tune below, you will see a sharp sign between each clef and the time signature.

Flat signs or sharp signs in this position are called key signatures.

This key signature shows a sharp sign on the treble clef F line.

This means that all the right hand Fs in the tune should be played as F sharps.

This sharp sign tells you to play F sharp in the left hand all the way through the tune.

The key signature is written on every new staff beside the clef...

...to remind you to keep playing F sharps instead of Fs.

Lullaby

Remember, this key signature means that you play all the Fs as F sharps in this tune.

In this tune, play F sharp with your second finger.

Starting again

In this tune, your right hand sometimes has to play two notes at the same time.

This is called playing a chord. Practise the chords separately before you play the tune.

The yodelling goat

Parts of bars

The time signature in the tune below tells you there are four beats in each bar. But the first bar only has two quavers in it.

This means it is only part of a bar. There are three crotchet beats missing.

A lot of tunes start with part of a bar. This is often called an upbeat.

Tunes that start with an upbeat finish with part of a bar too.

The last bar contains the missing beats from the first bar.

½ + ½ + 3 = 4

The beats in the first and last bars add up to make a whole bar.

Mallebrok

Count up the beats in the first and last bars of this tune. They add up to the top number of the time signature.

This is a Scandinavian tune. Look at the key signature. Play all the Bs as B flats.

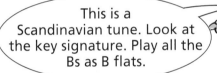

Hairpins

There are two new signs in the tunes on these two pages, < and >.

One tells you to get louder, the other to get quieter. Below you can see which is which.

One and a half beat notes

The next tune has a new note in it, called a dotted crotchet. Remember, a dot increases the length of the note by half as much again.

This is a dotted crotchet.

It lasts for a crotchet plus half a crotchet, which makes one and a half beats.

Clap and count these notes.

Say "and" for the half beat after the dotted crotchet.

Sarabande

A French tune: *Le coucou*

The name of this tune means "The cuckoo" in French.

The cuckoo has a special song, which you can hear in this tune wherever you see this:

Remember to take your fingers slightly off the keys when you come to a rest.

Make sure you play quietly where you see *p* and loudly where you see *f*.

Making up your own music

Do these two short tunes make you think of any particular things, places or sounds?

This one sounds like traffic.

This one sounds a bit like the sea.

Think of a sound, then play the piano in a way which reminds you of it. It could be a bird's song, like the cuckoo opposite.

It could be an animal sound, or a ride at the fair, or a stormy day.

You may need to play very high up...

Maybe you will find that playing a lot of notes at the same time is better.

See what happens when you use the foot pedals one at a time.

...or low down to find the right kind of sound.

Does it help you make the sound you want?

Now think of a mood, like happy, sad, angry or excited, and try to play notes which sound like that.

You may play something that sounds frightening or strange...

...or just funny.

When you have tried a few different sounds, why not link some of them together to make up your own music?

You could try making your music more interesting by playing it quickly, slowly, loudly or quietly.

You could ask a friend to guess what your music is about.

Tied together

There is a new sign called a tie in the next tune. When two notes are tied, you play one note lasting for the length of both notes. Notes of any length can be tied, but they must both be on the same line or space.

Click go the shears

26

Which notes?

Look at these notes. Can you remember all of their names? To help you remember which note is which, think back to the sentences you made up earlier. You can check your answers on page 32.

Cartwheels

Are you sitting comfortably?

A tricky tune: Crabs and snails

Make the crabs in the first half of the tune sound different from the snails in the second half. In the first half, take your fingers off the keys as soon as you have played them. This makes the notes sound short and spiky, like crabs running over rocks.

In the second half, hold the keys down right to the end of each note. This will make a smooth sound like sliding snails.

Quick quiz

What is this sign called and what does it do?

What sort of notes are these?

Does this sign tell you to get louder or quieter?

Check your answers on page 32.

Moving up the piano

When you play with another person, you often need to play your part higher up the piano so both of you have room to sit comfortably. You have to do this in *Sticky Cakewalk* on the opposite page.

Instead of starting on the E above Middle C, find the next E along on the right. Start playing there and pretend it is the E above Middle C. All the notes will sound higher than usual.

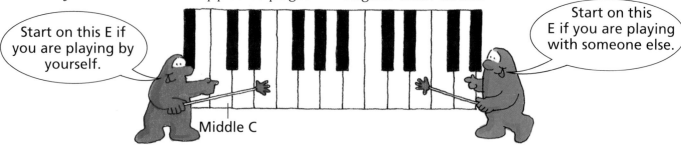

Start on this E if you are playing by yourself.

Start on this E if you are playing with someone else.

Middle C

Sticky Cakewalk (accompaniment)

This music is for your teacher or someone who is good at the piano to play.

It should be played at the same time as you play the tune on the opposite page.

A duet: *Sticky cakewalk*

This tune has quite a tricky rhythm. Clap
all the notes before you start so that
you know the rhythm when you
play the music.

If you want to play this tune with an accompaniment, look first at the opposite page.

A party piece: *Rondino*

Why not choose some of your favourite tunes to play to your family or friends?

Make sure you practise them all first.

GALWAY COUNTY LIBRARIES